Things on Wheels

by Tammy J. Schlepp

Copper Beech Books
Brookfield, Connecticut

Contents

© Aladdin Books Ltd 2000

Designed and produced by
Aladdin Books Ltd
28 Percy Street
London W1P 0LD

First published in
the United States in 2000 by
Copper Beech Books,
an imprint of
The Millbrook Press
2 Old New Milford Road
Brookfield, Connecticut 06804

ISBN 0-7613-1219-6

Cataloging-in-Publication data is on
file at the Library of Congress

Printed in U.A.E.

Coordinator
Jim Pipe

Design
Flick, Book Design and Graphics

Picture Research
Brian Hunter Smart

Wheels are everywhere!

See them on the street.

Spy them on the sidewalk.

They've even been to the moon!

Wheels can be big or small.

They can be used for work or play.

Bus

Buggy

What makes a wheel a wheel?

A wheel is shaped like a circle.

A wheel moves round and round.

A wheel is used for moving things.

How would you like a bicycle without wheels? It wouldn't move!

Bicycle

How does it move?

Skateboard

Look at these wheels on the skateboard and in-line skates.

What a lot of fun!

But there can be some bad falls too.

That's why it's smart to wear a helmet and padding.

In-line skates

Beetle

We have to push the pedals to get the wheels of a bicycle moving.

In a car or motorcycle, the engine does the work for us.

Cars are all shapes and sizes. The car above looks like a beetle.

Family car

A family car has a big trunk.

This red sports car can go fast.

Vroom Vroom! Those wheels can move!

Sports car

9

School bus

Can you see the wheels?

Lots and lots of people need to get to lots and lots of places.

People mover

Big cars and buses get this job done, and they use big wheels to help them do it.

11

Train

Where is the engine?

Hundreds of people can ride on a train at one time. Trains run on tracks, not roads.

Look at the special wheels they have. Today there are superfast trains that whiz along at great speeds.

Big trucks may have eighteen wheels
to help them carry heavy loads.

You need special training to drive a
truck this big.

Truck

The front part of the truck is called a cab.
That is where the driver sits.

The truck bends in the middle, so it can
turn in small spaces.

15

Fire trucks and ambulances must always be ready to go.

Fire trucks are painted red, so that it is easy to see them.

Ambulance

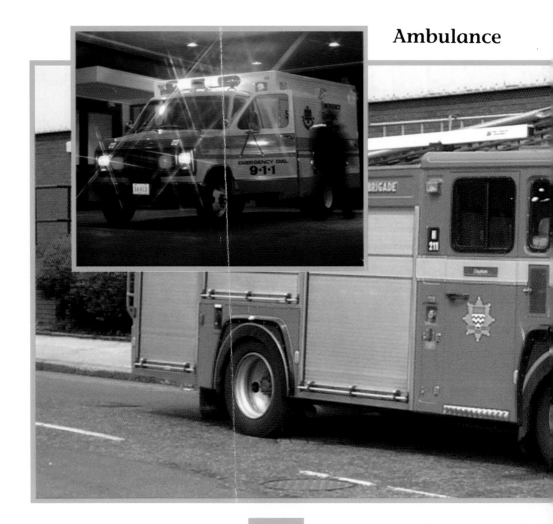

The flashing lights and wailing siren mean get out of the way. There is a fire or someone needs help, and we need to get there fast!

Our wheels are really rolling!

Fire truck

Sometimes a motorcycle goes to the rescue!

Motorcycle

Have you seen a digger with tracks?

A track is like a long belt that rolls over lots of wheels. Tracks make driving easy over bumpy ground.

Tracks

Tractor

See the ridges on these tires?
The ridges help the tractor
grip the ground.

Tires

They are like the studs on the
shoes of a baseball player that
keep the player from slipping.

Dump truck

This huge truck needs big strong
wheels to carry its heavy load.

The truck is so large, the driver has to climb up a ladder to get into the cab.

Big wheel

21

Some wheels are built
for speed.

Race cars have tires for dry
weather and other tires for
wet weather to help them
grip the track.

Racing car

Motorcycle race

Look at the wheels on these motorcycles.
Motorcycle racing is fast, noisy, and a little
scary too.

You can really get hurt in a fall!

23

There are even wheels in space!

The wheels on this buggy were made to ride over the rocky ground of the moon.

Moon buggy

This space shuttle is made to take off like a rocket and land on its wheels like a plane.

Space shuttle

Wheee! This machine on wheels has no driver. It's a roller coaster.

It rolls up, down, and upside down.

Want a good scream?
Climb on board!

Roller coaster

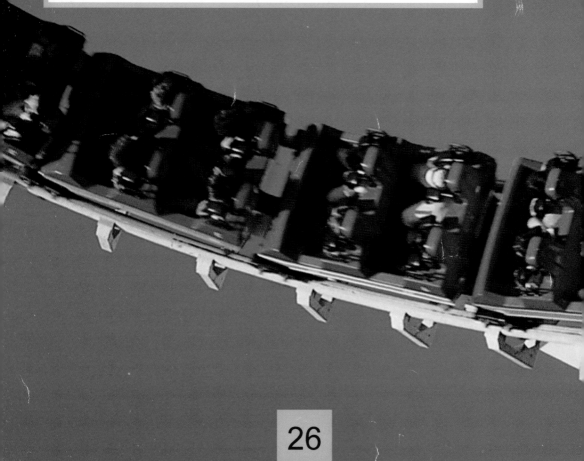

Can You Find?

This book is full of wheels, big and small, smooth and bumpy. Look for these wheels —where can you find them?

B

A

C

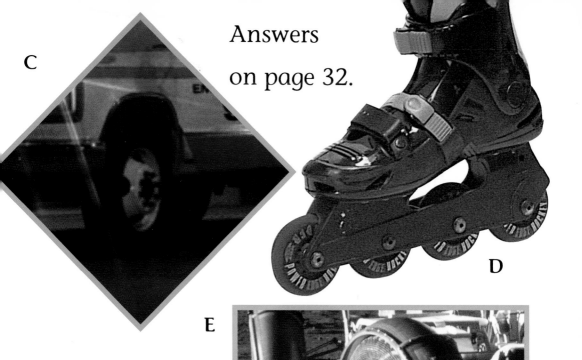

Answers
on page 32.

D

E

Clue: Look at
pages 5, 7, 14,
16, 19, and 24.

F

Do You Know?

People have been using wheels for thousands of years.

Do you know what these wheels are made of?

Bicycle wheels

Stagecoach wheels

Car wheels

Train wheel

Spacecraft
wheels

Answers on page 32.

Index

ANSWERS TO QUESTIONS

Pages 28-29 – **A** comes from a bicycle • **B** comes from a tractor • **C** comes from an ambulance • **D** comes from a pair of in-line skates • **E** comes from a moon buggy **F** comes from a truck.

Pages 30-31 – The first **bicycle wheels** were made of wood • **Stagecoach wheels** were made of wood • The first **car wheels** were made of wood • **Train wheels** are made of a metal called steel • **Spacecraft wheels** are made of light, strong metals.

Photocredits: Abbreviations: t-top, m-middle, b-bottom, r-right, l-left.
Cover, 1, 2ml, 2mr, 4, 5, 6, 12-13, 20, 21, 23, 26-27, 28l, 31mr—Digital Stock. 2tl, 7, 29tr—R. Vlitos. 2l, 3, 14-15, 29b—Scania. 8, 9 both, 11, 16-17, 22—Select Pictures. 10, 16l, 29t—Corbis. 18—John Deere. 19 both, 28r—Renault. 24, 25, 29mr—Stockbyte. 31b—NASA.
Illustrator: Peter Hutton, Alex Pang.